Hustling Backwards

The Struggles of a User

by Helen Robichaud

DORRANCE
PUBLISHING CO
EST. 1920
PITTSBURGH, PENNSYLVANIA 15238

Dorrance Publishing Co
585 Alpha Drive
Suite 103
Pittsburgh, PA 15238
Visit our website at *www. dorrancebookstore.com*

ISBN: 979-8-88812-454-3
eISBN: 979-8-88812-954-8

Hustling Backwards

The Struggles of a User

Acknowledgements

To list the names and give thanks to everyone who inspired a poem or helped me along the way would make a book in itself. But acknowledgements need to be given to Brittany Lore and Branden Denis for typing, Candice Tucker for helping create the cover, Julie Burns for typing, formatting and editing. To J.B. for inspiring the title, to M and T, hats off to you both, you know who you are. To Fred, my light and one love, and last but certainly not least, Emily, my daughter. It took me a lot longer than promised but you have never lost hope or stopped believing in me. I love you, Emily! Thanks for believing in me.

Life

Life is an opportunity, benefit from it - Life is beauty, admire it - Life is bliss, taste it - Life is a dream, realize it - Life is a challenge, meet it - Life is a duty, complete it - Life is a game, play it - Life is costly, care for it - Life is wealth, keep it - Life is love, enjoy it - Life is mystery, know it - Life is a promise, fulfill it- Life is sorrow, overcome it - Life is a song, sing it - Life is a struggle, accept it - Life is a tragedy, confront it - Life is an adventure, dare it - Life is luck, make it - life is too precious, do not destroy it - Life is life, fight for it!

-Mother Theresa

Dedicated in loving memory to my nephew

Christopher Mark Denis (Denny)

February 18, 1975 - June 2, 2003

DENNY

A nephew, a friend, a brother
You ask, "which one was he?"
We fought, we laughed, I cared for him,
To me he was all three.

As an aunt, I saw the pain
The struggle was often sad
He's programmed like his mother
But tried to be like dad

He was born when I was nine
And my duties soon began
To babysit and help him grow
Into a fine young man

I was still a kid you see
The responsibilities rough
So the role of being the auntie
Was sometimes quite too tough

As time went by
I became his friend
And he came to me oh so proud
Showing the things that he'd acquired
All to impress a crowd

I fought with him like a brother
Because of choices that he'd make
Selling drugs and playing with guns
Was more than I could take

I miss you oh so much
The ache deep in my heart

I wish that life was just a play
Because I'd give you another part

You were such a good man Christopher
Still learning to find your way
Then your life was taken from us
And for that he'll somehow pay

I know it's not for me to decide
The fate of that young man
But I don't understand God's reason
For increasing his lifespan

Your kids are awesome, Denny,
And not knowing you they'll regret
But as long as I am a part of their life
I'll never let them forget

Losing you was my demise
But I'm getting back on my feet
I went to prison for awhile
The experience kind of neat

I learned to write my feelings down
In words that sometimes rhyme
Life is three dimensional
The fourth dimensions time

Time is all we have on earth
And that's what we call life
It's not always the choices we make
Sometimes it's the luck of the dice

I'll see you again on the other side
And I'll wait with apprehension
Until that day comes, please be with me
During my fourth dimension

About the Author

1 was born in 1965, the youngest of seven. I was raised in a small mill town in southern Maine, where, like most mill towns, everyone knows everyone. Most of my life I fell into the shadows of my siblings, just one of the pack never standing out on my own. Always someone's little sister, the pot smoker, the rebel, the single one.

Along with most people, I have the issues, insecurities, and fears. They have influenced my decisions, fogged my judgment, and kept me from becoming my true self as God intended. It's a constant challenge of mine to remind myself that I am loved unconditionally by God, and if I do right by the life he has given me, then I will find the happiness I want.

My belief is that we all have mental health (mind), physical health (body), and spiritual health (soul), and if we can get our souls healthy, then we will find true happiness. I have written some stories that represent the struggles that I have gone through and am still going through to achieve the happiness that was intended for us all.

We've all been given the gift of life, some with a clear purpose, what we do with our lives is up to us. I want to personally show my thanks to God by becoming the best me that I can be.

I continue to strive for emotional wellbeing, and if I can inspire a few to focus on their emotional health and not just their physical and mental health, then, I will be living my purpose. (I think.)

The following poems have been collated to the best of my ability in the order in which they were written.

I was incarcerated from September 2006 until February 2008 on a probation revocation. After my nephew was killed, I began smoking crack in an attempt to deny my grief. I got into legal issues and was giving a short amount of time in the county and two years' probation. I decided not to report and hustle during my probation, trying to stack enough money for commissary, then turn myself in. Three months later, I was caught, and to remove myself from my circumstances, I asked the judge to revoke my probation which would allow me the opportunity to address my grief as well. Towards the end of my sentence, I enrolled in a creative writing class. In January 2008, I wrote my first poem, titled "Released."

The following eight poems were written during the last month of my incarceration.

Table of Contents

RELEASED

The taste of watermelon
The thickness of worry
So many things
That need to be buried

Time is ticking
For me to leave
Can that anxious pressure
Be gone please

Papers to write
Things to make
The friends I've made
With me I'll take

There's no other place
Where it's all about me
No job, no kids
No never-ending fees

Taking full advantage
To repair my wounds
My childhood scars
I'll release in balloons

A new beginning
Is awaiting me now
And that fear in my stomach
I can only say wow

It's like a music box
That's gone in for repair
A new timer, new tuning
A little adjusting of gears

When I walk out these doors
And just past the gates
May beautiful music
Be that what I make

SECOND CHANCE

Mixed emotions to say the least
Leaving some friends behind
You won't be forgotten, that's for sure
It's for you I'll be standing in line

To lobby, to preach, to speak my piece
To create a different way
To heal your wounds and mend the holes
In an alternative place to stay

Without the stamp of felon
To carry on us so bold
and for those of us that line don't apply
At least offer us parole

A chance to prove to you the change
With all the work we've done
Don't make us stay for what seems forever
For all the world to shun

We're beautiful women who've made a mistake
That pain we live with daily
But there once was a time in our lives
That we danced around so gaily

I know it's easy not to care
To deny us another glance
But God only knows the difference I'd make
If given a second chance

BEYOND THE GATES

The closeness of freedom
And ever present change
The things I want
Have such a wide range

Inventions to make
Politics to pursue
And every time I turn
I see a different view

I'm often told to do
One thing at a time
And in doing so
I'll have peace of mind

No need to worry
No need for bets
As long as God's with me
I'll never have to fret

Take one day at a time
It's an old cliché
But in doing so
I'll find my way

There's a world out there
That's waiting to see
The difference I can make
By just being me

MY SENTENCE

When I came to prison
The journey began in the pods
It was the end of male contact
For there were nothing but broads

Most women were white
Two Spanish, one black
I kept to myself
For fear I'd get smacked

Women are women
Some gay, some straight
Whatever they're choice
There is no reason to hate

One hour for rec
And half hour chows
To complete this journey
I prayed to God, "How?"

They lied and cheated, boasted and bragged
To create a faulty image
So afraid the truth would be seen
And we'd all notice the damage

Some of them were scared
And others constantly strut
I may be wrong about them all
Because the shields that they hold up

The lessons learned, the wisdom gained
In this chaotic place
I'll be forever grateful to all
But especially God's grace

The journey is for us all to take
To reverse in us the disgrace
When we leave this place, hold our heads up
And no longer hide our face

MENTORS

My three mentors
What is it I can say
Without your encouragement
I'd still be lost today

You've been there for me
Throughout my stay
Helping me identify
Finding my own way

To keep me focused
On my plight
To fight for justice
Instead of spite

I'll always reflect
Back on our talks
And emulate my mentors
Not just talk the talk

Advocacy, politics
Who knows what I'll do
I might just pass a law
Then again, maybe two

For rehabs and parole
I'll be fighting with will
For the friends I've left behind
To pass a bill on Capitol Hill

To repay those that have been so kind

MALCOLM

I'll always tell stories
Of the Malcolm shuffle
And the little things you do

Your dry sense of humor
And constant demeanor
That reinforces you true

"Medication ladies"
"Medication ladies"
Spoken at the end of our walks

Or the rare occurrence
To spend enough time
To appreciate one of your talks

You're a gift to the center
You must already know
And I speak on behalf of the gals

When you leave this place
It will be a disgrace
An unfortunate loss to us all

I smile when
I think of my time here
With you and Ross to boot

It wasn't all that bad
The time we all had
In fact it was quite a hoot

EMILY

Emily, Emily, Emily
Oh where do I begin
I guess I'll start from years ago
When I dreamed of you within

I dreamed of little girls
That I could dress with joy
But you kicked and screamed at every dress
For you wanted to be a boy

Michael Jordan was the one
That you always wanted to be
You couldn't have picked a better man
If wanting to be a he

You never wore pink or ruffles
For that would cause a fight
But you cried with me at movies
And cuddled with me at night

I always worry, Emily
Of the choices you will make
I pray every day that I did okay
Guiding the steps you take

You're a teenager now, that I can't change
And you'll probably want to rebel
I've been away for a while
And this you can clearly tell

Please don't be angry with me forever
To you I say, "I'm sorry"

And I'll be there for you whenever you need me
To assure you I'm still your mommy

A beautiful woman you're turning into
You're smart, loving, and bright
You're my prayers answered from long ago
I'm finally seeing the light

With all the pain I've caused you
I hope it all will mend
And we can build on our relationship
Becoming closer friends

Never forget that I'm your mom
For this I say is true
I thank our God every day
For blessing me with you

HEALED

I tried to cry
For "me" inside
But couldn't

I tried to cry
For "myself" inside
But wouldn't

I tried to cry
For the "I" inside
But thought I shouldn't

For the
Couldn'ts
Wouldn'ts
And
Shouldn'ts
I finally cried

I cried alive
Inside
Me, Myself, and I

On February 29, 2008, I was released. Because of government budget cuts, I was put on a waiting list for housing with nowhere to go. I moved in with my mom. On April 28, 2008, my mom died. I relapsed. I was now on my own, homeless, depressed, and addicted. The following poems were written over the next several years following my release and the death of my mother.

PLAYING THE GAME

Playing the game to pave the way
For a reputable lifestyle
That's here to stay

The happiness we want
is the American dream
That we all strive to acquire

But the chances are slim
And the opportunities grim
Yet we never give up the desire

To have the money
To pay our bills, go to the movies
Instead of pills

We sling dope and coke
To make a quick buck
And avoid the cops
With a smidgeon of luck

The addictions we have
Are due to a loss, be it
A death, abuse, or neglect
All we want is happiness and love
And maybe a little respect

The chances we take
Breaking the law
Is a risk we're
Willing to take

We pray everyday
For God's help as we play
And keep us this side of the gate

The systems fail us
Time and again
Our politics corrupt
From deep within

So we make our own way
Playing the game
Day after day we're stuck

Maybe someday I'll exit
This game
And make an honest buck

ON THE GRIND

Politics, systems,
Regulations and rules
Making life difficult
Not lending a clue

To be a success
And achieve happiness
Staying within the law

It's a difficult task
And I often ask
How do you make it alone

When you work 9-5
And your still way behind
You're sure to feel defeat

It's simple to take
The easy way out
And play the game
Of the streets

DEAR FRIEND

My dear friend
He's ornery as a bear
He acts like he don't like me
But I know he really cares

He calls on me for favors
And I jump at his command
I met him as a little boy
And now he's a young man

I argue with him often
It's often done in fun
I know I am a friend
But I feel like I'm his mom

He never is specific
About anything he does
You don't know where he's going
Not even where he was

He'll be my friend forever
For this I say is true
But having a friend like him
You'll never have a clue

VISIONS

Lack of knowledge
And direction to take
What to do next
For difference to make

To publish my poems
And have my words seen
I need the help of someone
Who knows what I mean

To create change for people
Who need another view
From the world of dysfunction
That keep us feeling blue

To get my words out there
Hoping to inspire a few
To change their lives
What can I do

I can never give up
For they all say it's right
To continue this journey
Is my God-given plight

APRIL

I'm sad he's gone
A month of bliss
To do it all over
I wouldn't want to miss

It was loving, romantic,
Sensual and bold
Making me warm inside
Never feeling the cold

He was the answer to my dreams
No one could deny
The passionate screams
You could see in my eyes

It was a short-lived romance
That month last spring
But I'll never regret
My moments with him

In the spring of 2008, I worked as a painter. I was at a job site when I met "F" and we began a friendship that I hoped blossomed into more, but I didn't rush it because I didn't feel worthy of him.

The reason for mentioning "F" was to create the time line and you will see in future poems the reason for doing this.

I met "E" through a friend of mine and he needed a place to stay. It was not a romantic thing between us, but we were both spiritual. My daughter was still with family, so being alone, it was nice having him around.

UNMASKED

Everything but touch
Is a lonely way
Together with someone
Day after day

Showing your soul
And willing to share
The struggles of life
That we all have to bear

My emotions are real
All I do is feel
The truth of myself
In this unforgiving world

I yearn for love
It's sometimes under my nose
But I'm often blinded
And there it goes

Looking for someone
To fill the holes
But God is the answer
At least that's what I'm told

E's View

A message from God
To stay in this place
And learn a new lesson
Without family grace

On my own,
Finding my way
Following God's lead
To enjoy my stay

I've met a few women
That don't have a clue
To have my love
They need to know you

I guide them and show them
With all of my heart
That there's a better way
If they only would start

To be true to themselves
In God's divine way
If I knew that they heard me
Then maybe I'd stay

I don't know what to do
I wait for a sign
The truth will be seen
All in good time

LEAVING

I feel the loss already
A friend that's gone away
I hope sometime I'll see you again
And maybe then you'd stay

I wonder if that's what I'd really want
To have you so close in my life
To see my mistakes and failures
Especially if you've found a wife

Not that that's what I'd want to be
for that I could not know
We were brought together briefly
Then it was time for you to go

I got mad at you so often
And defensive you made me
Condescending and patronizing
Telling me how I should be

Now that you're gone I'm realizing
What you say and do
It was a lesson to learn
Right from the start
To listen to God not you

I sometimes think
That he was the one
But I'm a lost soul
And now it's all done

Maybe someday
I'll see him again
And my heart and my head
Won't both be a spin

Who knows maybe then
I'll feel the embrace
Of the man that showed me
That I lost my faith

The touch of his lips
The feel of his hands
If it's God's will
I'll call him my man

LONELY

I want to sleep
To sleep it away
But I wake up to the same old
Feelings each day

The financial struggles
And the fact I'm alone
Just me and myself
In this cold, lonely home

Would winning the lotto
Make me all whole
Or would it feel lonelier
And much more cold

I remind myself often
That money's not the way
That it's God I need
In my life everyday

Most times I talk
But I don't walk the walk
Another day gone
There's a non-stopping clock

24 hours,
Again and again
Day in and day out
When will it end

The obstacles I face
Time and again
Will all disappear
When I make God my friend

OUR PRESIDENT

Barrack Obama
What can I say
I look forward to you
Paving the way

Hope and empowerment
You give to us all
I have faith in you
That you won't take the fall

For all your mistakes
That I'm sure you'll make
You're human after all
Not another fake.

To run this country
With us all in mind
The American Dream
We all want to find

I look forward to the change
That you promised us all
So we can hold our heads high
And walk very tall

If nothing more happens
In this four-year span
The change already took place
With you being our man

A STEP FORWARD

The image of life
What should it be
Love and happiness
And a spirit set free

I've been lost for awhile
But I'm finding my way
I struggle a lot
But I'm doing okay

Staying focused on me
To get it all right
I'll get there sometime
If I keep God in sight

To guide me and teach me
In his divine way
I'll learn the lessons I need
To be happy each day

I need to listen to him
When it's quiet inside
If I practice it daily
I won't have to hide

Hide from the fears
That I face everyday
But I won't have to do it
If I learn how to pray

CRISIS CARE

Sitting in the sun
Listening to tunes
Trying to get a tan
While I reflect on recent wounds

I worry how I'll survive
When I leave this place of refuge
The feeling I have in my stomach
Is just a little less the huge

So many people out there
That will try to steer me wrong
I need to think of my daughter
To hopefully keep me strong

She gets mad at me when I fail
Thinking that I don't care
Yet all I want is a home
Instead of the bullshit that I bear

I escape by getting high
So I don't feel my despair
But when the high is over
The feeling's right back there

"J"

My lover "J"
Your always on my mind
I wish that I could see you now
To spend a little time

You said to me if you knew me sooner
I would have been your girl
But I never stop hoping
To be the only one in your world

We never had the chance to see
What life could be alone
We always had to rent a room
In someone else's home

You never saw the side of me
That stayed at home and watched T.V.
I might cook pasta, chicken, or steak
Or maybe something sweet to bake

Either way you'll see me soon
Make love all night and sleep till noon
To wake up with you next to me
In my own bed at peace I'll be

I dream of making love to you
Every day of the week
To share that kind of life with you
I'd love to have a peek

To think I'll always be second
Saddens me to no end
I don't think my heart could handle
Only being your good friend

If that's the way it has to be
I'll have to harden my heart
But please remember my dear sweet J
You've had me from the start

After "E" moved, I spent a few months alone. An old friend that I had feelings for and use to hustle with and get high with was doing a short bid in prison. I started writing to him and I thought that we would rekindle what we had upon his release, which was a week before my birthday, but he never showed, so on my birthday, I went out with a girlfriend of mine and it was that night that I met "T," a dysfunctional relationship to say the least.

NEW LOVE

I want to say I love you
But I'm afraid you'll go away
So I keep my feelings to myself
In hopes that you will stay

As time goes by my weakness shows
I try to be so strong
I never want you thinking
That being with me is wrong

My heart is big and full of love
And to you I want to give
To give to you my heart and soul
Being happy as we live

I'm so afraid that the mistakes I've made
Will make you want to leave
If you did I'd suffer the loss
And again I'd have to grieve

The way you show me that you care
With all the things you do
Gives me faith that you are real
And all you say is true

I finally feel I'm not alone
With my childhood fears at bay
You make me happy and keep me smiling
Each and every day

FURNISHING

I'm accused of being shady
When all I do is try
To make the ones around me
Enjoy themselves a high

I do my best with what I have
And still look out for me
But it never seems to be enough
Therefore I won't be free

Free from stinking-thinking
And suspicious minds alike
Sometimes I'd like to tell them all
To take a fucking hike

If they really think the worst of me
Then why do they choose me
Could it be that I'm the one
Who can always make it be?

If I choose to stop this game
Will the relationships stay the same
Or would the ones so close to me
Eventually forget my name?

INSECURE

All it takes is a phone call
To put me in a mode
Paranoid and jealous
As scenarios in my mind unfold

Why do I feel so insecure
Why do I feel so defensive
When I really don't know the extent of the call
Yet I always slip into offensive

I analyze and stay on guard
To protect my heart and image
To save myself the humiliation
Of being punked out first

So I put on the front that I do not care
While I quietly hurt inside
Why's it so much easier
Than sacrificing pride

"T"

Sitting on my boyfriend's stoop
Wondering where he is
Where he is doesn't matter
It's who that makes me scared

He says that he'll be there for me,
But it's hard for me to trust
Especially when he's not around
My heart begins to crush

I hold my breath when I'm scared or mad
It's a reflex I don't understand
Cuz I really thought that he would be
My forever man

We have so many things in common
T.V. shows, games, and food
But I guess I'm not the special one
That puts him in the mood

Then I hit survivor mode
And vicious I can be
He's a self-righteous hypocrite
Who is he to talk to me

Talking to me like I'm a charity case
Pisses me off to no end
I just wish that he'd stop playing me
And truly be a friend

MISTAKES

An obligation to a friend
That's what I felt back then
I didn't want to let him down
So I agreed to fuck his friend

He gave me crack after the fact,
And it made me feel so cheap
The only thing that gave me peace
Was that he was no creep

Four years later I'm paying the price
Because I was honest with my man
Now he thinks that I'm a whore
And that I cannot stand

How does one erase the past
Or at least, put it behind you
When a question's asked, do you lie
Or is it better to be true

I've always believed what they say
That the truth will set you free
I now believe that's not the case
Cuz again it's only me

HONESTY

You look at me with disgust
It's anger that I feel
For you to always be that way
Is a fate I don't want sealed

You tell me that I'm lying
When the truth is being told
For you to believe in everyone else
Is getting kind of old

I'm really feeling at a loss
For what to say or do
Regardless of what I choose
You'll never think it true

I wish that you would be the man
And step up to the plate
And make demands with us both in mind
Before it's all too late

I'm so tired of being the one
That's left to make the call
Because, if it's wrong, in your eyes
My backs against the wall

If you could put me in your arms
And refuse to let me go
I'd feel a lot more like a couple
And then you'd see me glow

I'd glow with pride that you're by my side
Through the thick and through the thin
And please remember my righteous one
That we all were born with sin

Can we forgive, can we forget
And put it all behind us
Or are we stuck in this vicious circle
Of never feeling trust

SECRETS

He keeps his life so private
How do I learn to trust
When all his friends are female
Was it love or was it lust

He says that he loves me
Yet he doesn't share his past
If we can't live in the present
How will it ever last

His life is none of my business
That fact I must accept
But to live this life so blindly
Is a thought my mind rejects

I feel it isn't right
To be kept so in the dark
When it comes to me I give to him
The ammo to break my heart

I try to shut my mouth
So he might know how it feels
But apparently he doesn't care
Cuz he just digs in his heels

I assume it's insecurity
That makes him keep his past
Just in case our love don't work
He won't go back to last

Last in line to find the love
Love's what we want at least
But love will never come to be
When your past is on a leash

A leash for you to pull on
When time with me gets tough
It doesn't help the relationship
In fact it gets more rough

Will he ever trust me enough
To finally let me in
Or will I be left on my own
To find out what's under his skin

I sit here by his side
Not knowing what to say
Questioning whether his love for me
Will allow me another day

I'm afraid to ask about anything
For fear I'll get depressed
So I choose to live in silence
And continue an occasional guess

DISPENSABLE

I can't believe he'd be so mean
As to actually throw me out
It seems he's had some other plans
That he won't willingly discount

He expects for me to allow him in
And devote myself completely
But his women, his friends, and his little world
Are kept away from me so neatly

I'll accept that we're all done
And move ahead on my own
Maybe someday you'll learn to share your world
But not till you're fully grown

As big as you are it's hard to believe
Your heart can be so cold
When you claim to love me time and again
At least that's what I'm told

You're a selfish person, "T," that I now can see
Why we were together so long
We wasted less than a year, I shouldn't complain
In fact you've made me more strong

BAILING

People leave cuz it's easier than solving their disputes,
a coward's way if you ask me, then accepting a little guilt.

Knowing that it takes two for a fight to even be,
If the love is really true, why do they always flee?

They escape the pain and transfer the blame, for it's easier that way,
Heaven forbid they do what they said, and remain right next to me.

They close the door behind them, it's abandonment that I feel,
I felt it my whole lifetime, is it fear or is it real?

I guess it's true, what they say, you can only count on yourself,
To deal with the ups and downs, with the cards that you've been dealt.

Alone again I find myself in a world that feels so dark,
I lose my faith in others, I should have learned right from the start.

God is the only one that loves me to the core,
l never thought that loving me was such a difficult chore.

A chore that no one seems to want, for that I don't know why,
I guess it's harder work for them, than simply saying bye.

I open up to those I love, but it's apparently not enough,
For them to see the real in me, and stop packing their stuff.

If that's the way it's gonna be, I guess it won't be them,
I want someone to stand by me, through the thick and through the thin.

After "T" bailed on our relationship, I moved on. I continued my rollercoaster ride trying to get on my feet and find love and security. I have spent a lot of time looking outside of myself to find happiness. I had insignificant romances with a few different men and was still fighting addiction. I came to realize that I have one man that does care, "F." He has been there for me since I met him, but because of my low self-worth, I didn't believe in the potential of us being together, so things were kept casual. "F" has been there for me throughout my struggles, sharing intimacy without judgment thus allowing me to take this path without the fear of losing him. He has been where I am and knows the struggles I face. That has helped me understand that I'm not alone, despite my feelings of loneliness.

HOMELESS

Nine months homeless
And trying to survive
Everyone's a risk to me
I can't believe my eyes

The ones that try to help me
Don't realize they have a part
Trying to fix my circumstances
But what's broken is my heart

My heart doesn't heal from getting work
To hustle with my friends
It only keeps me down and out
From the rocks I tend to lend

I believe that they'll do me right
Because the friend they pose to be
But the addicts there, and not the friend
Who suffers now is me

I suffer now cuz I'm in debt
To the one that gives me work
He seems to think it's easier
To take with it and twerk

But as a user it's hard to see
The opportunity to do just me
Doing me is hard you see
Because my friends are users
Just like me

I want to stop smoking rock
And get on my feet
But what I fear is loneliness
And feeling always beat

After five days now of crisis care
Will it all begin to mend
And can I keep all that I have
And still make it to the end.

The end of this game we play
Hustling drugs day after day
Hopefully finding the courage
To walk the other way

The other way is far from here
It seems forever and a day
To make the change last lifetime
I need to learn to pray

Pray for help everyday
To see the real in me
And not be afraid to show the rest of you
What God plans for me to be

DESIRES

I worry about the friends I've made
In this world of drug addiction
They all feel the same deep down
To be true to they're convictions

Wanting a better life for themselves
And the ones that they love
Hoping they find their peace of mind
I pray to God above

As I emerge from this life of drugs
I'll leave them all behind
And proceed with my mission to help
Others find mended hearts and clear minds

I hope I'll never lose them
But it's inevitable I think
Cuz I can't live a life of hypocrisy
By continuing to use in that rink

Maybe I'll see them again
And it won't be part of the hustle
We'd be sharing healthy lifestyles
Being kings and queens of our castles

I know that's wishful thinking
But hopeful is what I am
Naive and optimistic
Describes me to the end

STUCK ON STUPID

Stuck on stupid
The only way to describe
The feeling you get
When you always get high

Putting off things
You should do everyday
Quality time with your kids
The most important I'd say

Accomplishing nothing
To say the least
Losing yourself to the drugs
What a beast

The light in the tunnel
Can we see the end
We try everyday
But there's always a bend

To achieve our goals
And remain quite lucid
Stay straight and focused
Not stuck on stupid

OPTIMISTIC

Sitting in my room
Alone at night
The prospects of love
Nowhere in sight

T.V. and music
My only companion
Night after night
I feel so abandoned

Learning to love myself
Is a constant challenge
But someday I'll get it,
And it will be my salvage

I'm often told
I'm a diamond in the rough
But to polish that gem
Is often tough

I'll get there someday
All in good time
And from that day forward
I'll continue to shine

HOPE

I'm proud of myself
I told my friends
I'm done with the pipe
This is the end

The end of the guilt
That I feel all the time
A new beginning
I'm starting to shine

No more disappointing
The ones that care
For the last time hopefully
I'm clearing the air

I want a fresh start
But I'm afraid of a fall
When I feel the temptation
I'll just make a call

When boredom sets in
I'll know what to do
I'll remember the talks
That I shared with you

DETACHED

Detached is a word that comes to mind
When I think of my body and soul
My body is visible for all to see, but
My soul feels like a hole

To have the knowledge but not believe
In the qualities that I have,
Gives me a life that's superficial, it's
No different than a disease

Trying to learn to reprogram myself
From the childhood scars I've endured
It's not as easy as staying away from a flame
When I know that I'll get burned

To repair my soul I need to believe
In the person I am inside
If I love myself then I'll heal myself and
I'll finally stop looking outside

I need to clear the clutter,
That creates for me a fog,
That clouds my judgment day after day,
What I need is the guidance of God

To help me see the good in me
That I know I've always had,
And stop this vicious circle
Of always feeling bad

I picture my soul in colors
It helps to keep me whole
My favorite colors are purple and green,
And different shades of gold

These colors glow inside me,
If I look to them I'll see,
And be connected body and soul,
And finally be set free

"W"

It began with a shotgun
And the slip of a tongue
And I knew it would be my undoing.

Chemistry was strong
The desire was real
The fantasies in my mind were spewing

An unhealthy attraction
To say the least
You see, I'm wanting to be
Ravaged all night by this beast

A beast with a bite
That hurts to the core
That's why it's unhealthy
Cuz I'm begging for more

More of the passion
That I felt that night
But he stops in for a moment
Then he's gone out of sight

It angers me that he
consumes my thoughts
Cuz the feelings are one sided

My logic tells me to let it go
Before my heart and my head
Are collided

DOGGED

When I first met this man
I felt the desire
To know him and do him
All I felt was the fire

I followed my heart
Instead of my head
Now I'm kicking myself
Cuz I'm 200 in debt

I'm bummed cuz I liked him
And the passion seemed real
Now he's gone from my life
Like it's no big deal

It's a big deal to me
The 200 was rent
I put faith in this guy
He seemed like a gent

I was feeling this guy
The excitement was real. I still can't believe.
He'd intentionally steal

He stole my heart briefly
At least it was quick
But it hurts all the same
Like you've just been bit

Bit by a wolf
It hurts to the core

Time will heal everything
But I'm still feeling sore

Grimy is not how
He wants to be known
Yet that's all that I think of
My mind's just been blown

Blown by the thought
Of what it could be
If he'd had half a conscience
And thought something of me

Playing with dogs
I'm sure to get bit
Now that fire inside me
Is no longer lit

TRANSPARENT

Fucking off is
Not being true to oneself
Diverting your focus
From the feelings you've felt

Is it the answer
It's a short lived fix
But it's all a disguise
And its life that we miss

The truth is all masked
By the things we do
When we're fucking off
It's not the real you

It's the face that we put on
Time and again
When you've been through it
You've found a true friend

A true friend will see
The pain we hide
And will want to see
That one inside

That person we are
When we're not fucking off
Being transparent like that
You can't stay lost

PROMISES

What is a promise
Is it a vow
It's when your actions and words
Are both standing tall

I've always been told
That they're meant to keep
And when they are
I'm touched real deep

But when they're broken
It makes me cry
And I often say to myself,
"Why?"

Why do I let them
Affect my heart
It's because I had faith in them
Right from the start

Am I mistaken
To try once again
To call that person
My friend 'til the end

Answer me God,
It's you I ask
Am I right or is it
Just another task

I'm taught to forgive
But at what cost
Whatever way
It seems a loss

I lose myself
Or lose my friend
Confused and bewildered
When will it end

It ends with a promise
To not make that vow
A lesson learned
And for that I say, "Wow."

THE GAME

Don't hate the player
Hate the game
Cuz if you do so often
You'll face the shame

It's a grimy life
That you're forced to live
With the bottom-feeders
That give, give, give

If you want the paper
It's still the same
You're always in contact
When you're playing the game

It's survival of the fittest
When you're on the street
Watching your back
So you don't get beat

Beat by the players
They're so easy to hate
When you're trying to make the play

You see it's all the same
When you're on the streets
But it's more commonly known as the game

MY ROCK

My rock doesn't take the form
Of something for my head
It's strong, black, and sexy
For me my rock is Fred

He's been there before
And knows what's ahead
And understands the struggles
And the feelings that I dread

I look to him as my only friend
That tries to steer me right
And because the love I feel for him
I won't put up a fight

A fight that I'd be sure to lose
For myself as well as him
And instead of light ahead
That vision would be dim

I want to see me polished
Like a gem that's all aglow
Not caught up in a crack house
Feeling ashamed to let me show

I've always kept my weaknesses
From being seen by him
Yet I want him proud to be a part of me
Through thick and through thin

I want my rock to see me true
Being true to my word
But I'm mostly frozen by the fear
Of being kicked to the curb

SHAME

A disappointment to myself
That's what I am tonight
The inability to say no
To the demon of the pipe

It's a short lived high
That I should always avoid
And really is not that great
It causes shame and constant guilt
And that I definitely hate

Damage controls not needed tonight
Cause my money wasn't spent
But the feelings still the same
The constant need for repent

I disappoint my friend as well
For that I'm truly sorry
But sorry doesn't fix the deed
It's the friendship loss I worry

Not the drugs or the façade
Of what I think is real
I stupidly act in control
Like it's really no big deal

It is a big deal
To the ones I love
To keep a promise told
Sticking to my convictions
So not to feel the cold

The cold inside
That I want to hide
Is easy to avoid

Stay away from the pipe
The need for a light
And life can be enjoyed

My attentions diverted
From time with you
If only for a while
But I'd rather have an intimate moment
And share with you a smile

EPIPHANY

I've been told that I'm a rock
That I'm a survivor and I'm strong
I've discovered that there's another view
That couldn't be more wrong

I guess I'm seen by others
As a trigger to their drug
And I carry a reputation
Of gaming with the thugs

I can't believe it took so long
For me to see the facts
That it's crack they see instead of me
And my soul picks up the slack

The epiphany saddens me
That a death derailed me forever
The person I was before that day
Is something I can't recover

It's time for me to recreate
To recreate for you a view
I'll still be a strong survivor
But the rest will be all new

I pray for strength to accomplish this task
It seems so far away
To walk the walk instead of talk
And God be with me, I pray

FEAR

Admitting that I'm disabled
To an emotion feels so wrong
I used to be resilient
And viewed as being strong

I felt that strength in me
Since being a young girl
Thinking that I could make a difference
And change this fucked-up world

I think of names like Ghandi
And Martin Luther King
Then I think I'm crazy
Comparing myself to them

But then I think of celebrities
And the things they try to fix
With the passion that I feel inside
Maybe I too can do this.

The fears I face to take that step
Will always block my way
But not taking that step will set me back
And forever here I'll stay

I believe I have a gift
That really should be shared
But not succeeding with this plight of mine
Is something I couldn't bear

Gaining control of my issues
Is a struggle in itself
But now I think it's time for me
To live the life that I've been dealt

No matter what that path is for me
I have to take that step
To get beyond the walls of fear
That have always kept me back

I moved into a friend's place on top of the block, up the street from the projects. I stayed there for several months, and quite honestly, it was traumatizing to say the least, however, I did find time to write the three following poems.

GIRLS LOST

I never realized the depth
Of dysfunction until
Dealing with the girls

Tricks, hoes, and chicken heads
Caught up in their fucked up worlds

We see them on the streets
And sometimes in a trap
But they were once our little girls
Can you imagine that

What happened to their innocence
I often ponder the thought
Are they there seeking the drugs
Or the love they never got

I'd like to help them all
I see the beauty in each one
To provide a place of solace
But would they ever come

It scares me that these
Girls I've met, won't ever
Make it out
I know that they can do it
But their heads are full of doubt

Full of doubt and low self-worth
Just working what they've got
Believing in themselves I guess
Was something never taught

DRAMA

The violence I've seen is
Like none before
body parts bruised.
and heads feeling sore

Tempers rise and
Conflicts occur
But the reasons are
Sometimes the next day a blur

Uptown, downtown
And various others all around
Being all fucked up
Troubles sure to be found

We often fall short
Cuz someone planted a seed
And when the phone rings
There's another dirty deed

A dirty deed that someone
Wants to have done
So I'm off in a moment
But it's really no fun

He said, she said
Who's right, who's wrong
It doesn't really matter
Now that somebody's gone

Gone to the hospital
Nabbed by the cops
But when you get through it
You're feeling on top

Wrong time, wrong place
Some say it's Karma
But living the bullshit
Is nothing but drama

THE EVICTION

I sit here confused
Not knowing what to do
Trying to hold it together
But what I need is glue

I'm seeing the psychosis
From lack of sleep and drugs
Some of them are social
But most of them are thugs

I'm nervous when I'm home
And also when I'm not
The ability to protect my kids
Is something I ain't got

I'll go to sleep tonight
Not knowing of our fate
will we be forced to move from here
In less than forty-eight

I'm worried for my friend as well
The weight is on her back
She has to go to civil court
With a warrant on top of that

I got off the block, got a job, and I've been moving forward since.

65

"F"

I finally said I love you
To a man I've known for years
And when he said it back to me
It relinquished all my fears

Now he has to move away and
It saddens me to the bone
It's hard for me to imagine him
Not being close to home

He's been there for my joy and
Also for my tears
Giving me his comfort
And constant display of care

He's going to where there's family
And that I understand
But I can't stop the anxiety
Of losing my favorite man.

He's brought smiles to my face
With just the mention of his name
And guided me with wisdom to
Understanding this fucked up game

He represents the light to me
In a tunnel that feels so dim
I'd hoped when I got through it
I'd be blessed by God with him

I feel as though that tunnel closed
The light seems far away
Cuz there's nothing that I can do
To make him want to stay

I always have had the fantasy that
I'd someday be his girl
Being his significant within
This fucked up world.

GAYLE

I'm at a loss for words
I don't know what to do
Beginning a new job
To care for someone new

She goes by the name of Gayle
And she's a pleasure to be around
She thinks that things go missing
Then imagine that "they're found"

Celebrating a birthday just
A few days ago
DVD player and jewelry
And a bedazzle in the throw

One minute I'm her friend
The next I become her foe
I'll learn not to bring kielbasa
So I can see her glow

She glows with joy and happiness
Almost all the time
But when she's sad or scared
It could easily make you cry

I'll try to keep her happy
And most important keep her health
But when she's in rare form
I'll try to practice stealth

All we want for our girl Gayle
Is health, happiness, and love
And for her to have a rich full life
We pray to God above

DISTANCE

I'm finally moving forward
With a job and place to stay
But I still feel sad and lonely
Cuz my man's so far away

I have some friends around me
And their company I enjoy
But it can't replace the pleasure
Of me hanging with my boy

I'll see him very soon
And I'll snuggle in his arms
Then again he'll be gone from me
And I'll no longer feel that calm

The calm that he instills in me
Whenever he's in my reach
Will diminish to the phone calls
All I can do is hear him speak

It's not the same as feeling his touch
And I know that bothers him too
But the thought of being without him
I'd rather have the flu!

It makes me sad to say goodbye
To the man I love so much
Cuz from that point forward I'll be alone
And dream only of his touch

WHY

How could someone do that?
Is a question I often ask
And do they do it with intent
Then seek shelter behind a mask?

They promise and swear to
While they're telling a lie
And they sit up all indignant and right
Being selfish opportunist
How do they sleep at night

I get cynical sometimes
When people let me down
Is it just the ones around me, no
They exist in every town

"M"

I have a friend that cares for me
I really think it's true
He says he wants to help me
But we both have different views

Some of us are structured
And others of us aren't
To recognize that fact in me
Is something he ain't got

I'm not quite sure what to think
Cuz I'm living under his roof
And I'm not sure what's expected
When communication is aloof

I want to prove to him
That I am worthy of his help
But does he really believe in me
Or is it just a card that I've been dealt

What I need is structure
To accomplish all my plans
Not someone giving up on me
Especially this man

JUST ONE MORE

I don't want this book
To end with "M"
So one more time
I'll pick up this pen

I'll end this book
On a different note
And see where it takes me

If it helps someone else
Then it helps me
And hopefully at peace
Is where I'll be

Putting addictions at bay
With this turn on my track
To live my life righteous
No more talking smack

I sit here and ponder
what happens next
As this portion of my journey
comes to a close
Will I succeed, will I fail
It's all up to me
That I know

HUSTLING BACKWARDS

Hustling backwards
Are stories about me
And the roller coaster ride
Trying to get free

Some days I was focused
And others were a waste
Not doing what I should have done
Cuz I got caught up in the chase

Some poems are inspirational
And some are off the chain
But mostly recognizable
If you've ever played the game

The game is just a part of it
Emotional baggage is too
But if any of it sounds familiar
Then it may be a reflection of you